THE THIRD DECADE

TURNER WATERCOLOURS 1810–1820

005256

005256

DIANE PERKINS

The Third Decade

TURNER WATERCOLOURS 1810–1820

TATE GALLERY

Cover
Naples, the Castel dell'Ovo 1819
detail (cat. no. 46)

ISBN 1 85437 032 4
Published by order of the Trustees 1990
for the exhibition of 31st January–1st April 1990
Copyright © 1989 The Tate Gallery All rights reserved
Designed and published by Tate Gallery Publications,
Millbank, London SW1P 4RG
Typeset in Monophoto Baskerville
Printed by Balding + Mansell Limited, Wisbech, Cambs
on 150gsm Parilux Cream

Contents

Foreword

This is the third exhibition in our annual series surveying Turner's output of drawings and watercolours decade by decade. It covers the palmy years of Turner's career, when, despite some vigorous criticism, he enjoyed his richest measure of personal happiness and professional success. During this decade he painted many of the pictures that future critics would regard as consummate statements, whether of classical landscape, English pastoral, continental scenery or history ancient and modern. In these he summed up the achievements and interests of the first half of his career, while in drawings and colour studies he was anticipating the breadth of vision and the tonal and atmospheric concerns of his later work. It is Turner the traveller who emerges most clearly from this exhibition – whether in England, where he was making drawings for series of engravings such as *Picturesque Views on the Southern Coast*, as well as beautifully spontaneous studies from nature like the oil sketches he made in Devonshire in 1813, or in continental Europe where he was again able to travel freely after the Napoleonic War. We conclude our display with a fine group of the drawings and watercolours Turner made during his first visit to Italy in 1819.

The exhibition has been selected and catalogued by Diane Perkins, who is grateful for the help she has received from Cecilia Powell, one of our two Volkswagen scholars currently working on aspects of the Turner Bequest. Special thanks are due to the anonymous private collector and the Guildhall Art Gallery, who have kindly lent works to complement our own holdings in the Bequest.

Nicholas Serota *Director*

Introduction

The period 1810–1820 was for Turner one of professional triumph and personal contentment. It was also a time of controversy, but Turner now towered over his critics and continued unchecked in the development of his art. Projects and commitments initiated earlier in his career matured in these years, and he embarked on a wide range of new ventures. The decade saw not only a synthesis and consolidation of his ideas in a number of important exhibited pictures, but also a mounting anticipation of the concerns of his later work. By the time Turner arrived in Italy for the first time in 1819, he had reached a watershed; mingled with his excitement at finally seeing the places of which he had so long dreamed, was the knowledge that he was ready for change. He had reached a point from which he could only propel himself forward; his art would not be the same again.

Turner had begun the decade with a strong sense of purpose, determined both to clarify and communicate his ideas. In 1811, he delivered his first series of lectures as Professor of Perspective at the Royal Academy. He had delayed lecturing since his appointment in 1807, during which time he made careful preparations and produced many large scale drawings. His desire to glean as much information as possible on subjects related to his art is evident in the wide ranging content of the lectures which were designed to offer much more than merely mechanical instruction; they discussed the application of perspective rules to the wider interests of art, meditated on art history and offered a powerful statement of the moral value of Turner's own field of landscape painting.

Turner was also increasingly turning to poetry to elucidate the ideas behind his art. When, also in 1811, he embarked on a series of drawings to be engraved as *Picturesque Views on the Southern Coast of England*, he also began his most ambitious single poem yet, a long account of a tour of the south-west, juxtaposing scenic description with historical reflection and the patriotic moralising appropriate in wartime. This he perhaps hoped to adapt as an accompanying text to the engravings, and the association between his art and poetry was more publicly announced in 1812, when 'Snow Storm: Hannibal and his Army crossing the Alps' (B&J 126) was exhibited at the Royal Academy with the first of a succession of quotations from his 'Manuscript Poem', *Fallacies of Hope*. The 'Snow Storm' was among the most prophetic of the series of masterpieces Turner painted during this decade; its turbulent effects anticipate much later pictures. Other paintings seem more traditional and retrospective in mood as Turner continued his earlier exploration of the old masters; from this period sprang a series of tributes to Claude in such accomplished landscape paintings as 'Crossing the Brook' (B&J 130) and in scenes of classical mythology and history such as 'Apullia in search of Apullus' (B&J 128). Two of his most important paintings of the decade, 'Dido building Carthage' (B&J 131) and the 'Decline of the Carthaginian Empire' (B&J 135) were bequeathed by Turner in his will of 1829, to hang in perpetuity between two works by Claude in the National Gallery. Turner's concern for modern history was proclaimed in his 'Field of Waterloo' (B&J 138), a tragic rather than a triumphant vision of the aftermath of battle, again supported by poetic allusion, this time by a quotation from the third Canto of Byron's *Childe Harold's Pilgrimage*.

Turner, in common with many writers and artists of his generation, visited the battlefield. He made a tour of Belgium, the Rhineland and Holland in 1817, and material gathered on this trip was used for one of the supreme masterpieces of his middle years, the 'Dort or Dortdrecht, the Dort Packet-Boat from Rotterdam becalmed' (B&J 137). This picture, alike a celebration of the experience of travel, and an emulation of two other painters, the Dutch master, Aelbert Cuyp and Turner's contemporary, Augustus Callcott, marked a turning point in his career. While acknowledging the past, its breadth and luminosity looked forward to the future.

Turner's innovations, especially in matters of colour, tone and painterly effects, did not always please critics and connoisseurs, and hostile comments continued to be aimed at Turner from William Hazlitt and his old adversary, Sir George Beaumont, among others.

His concern to broaden the scope of his art can also be seen in his interest in architecture during this period. He designed a villa for himself, Sandycombe Lodge, in Twickenham, built between 1812 and 1813, and devised the plans for the building of an enlarged gallery at his London house in Queen Anne Street. His capacity to try his hand at a variety of endeavours was admired by John Constable who commented, after sitting next to Turner at an Academy dinner in 1813; 'I was a good deal entertained with [him]. I always expected to find him what I did. He has a wonderful range of mind'.

It was during this decade that Turner undertook a series of important engraving commissions which provided the impetus for the production of great quantities of drawings and over a hundred finished watercolours, made specifically for the purpose of being engraved. He continued to publish his series of characteristic mezzotints, the *Liber Studiorum*, until

1819, in addition to the proposals from engravers and publishers for topographical series. These publications continued to occupy him throughout the 1810s and necessitated his making frequent journeys around Britain.

The first commission of this kind was for Cooke's *Picturesque Views on the Southern Coast of England*. Turner travelled to the West Country on two (or possibly three) occasions during the early years of the decade, in order to collect material for the project. As well as the beautiful finished watercolours which resulted from the tours, he also made some unusual oil sketches of Devonshire scenery. Further material for the *Southern Coast* was gathered in Sussex, where he was engaged in making drawings for a group of watercolours for the local M.P., Jack Fuller; some of these were engraved by Cooke for his *Views in Sussex*.

He made annual visits to Yorkshire throughout the decade, staying at Farnley Hall, near Leeds, with Walter Fawkes, who proved to be his greatest patron during this period as well as an intimate friend. Fawkes commissioned Turner to make numerous watercolours of his house and grounds, and views of local scenery, as well as a series of bird drawings and illustrations of his collection of Civil War relics, the 'Fairfaxiana'. In 1816, Turner set out from Farnley on a longer tour of Yorkshire and Lancashire to make drawings for another important publication, *The History of Richmondshire*, for which he produced some of the most exquisite finished watercolours of his career. Further commissions for engraved series resulted in journeys to Durham and Scotland.

It was Fawkes who acquired the entire series of bodycolour sketches of Rhine subjects which Turner worked up from his 1817 tour of the Rhineland. In style and technique, the series is close to many of the views of Yorkshire scenery made for Fawkes at about the same time. In 1819, approximately sixty or seventy drawings by Turner from Fawkes's collection were included in an exhibition at his London house in Grosvenor Place, where they met with great acclaim.

In 1818, Turner had made a series of Italian views for James Hakewill's *Picturesque Tour in Italy*, basing his designs on the author's own drawings. It was not until the following year that Turner made what was perhaps the most important tour of his career – his first visit to Italy. Sir Thomas Lawrence, Turner's friend and compatriot, who was painting in Rome in 1819, had anticipated the impact such a visit would have on Turner's art, and wrote to Joseph Farington; 'Turner should come to Rome. His Genius would here be supplied with new Materials, and entirely congenial with it'. The beauty of the Italian landscape and the classical buildings of Rome and the Campagna would have been familiar to him from his knowledge of the work of earlier masters, such as Claude, Richard Wilson and Piranesi, and he naturally wished to see them for himself.

In Italy he produced some two thousand drawings, ranging from slight pencil memoranda in his small sketchbooks to larger designs in water-colour or bodycolour. He does not seem to have worked in oil during this tour and his object was to learn, observe and compile a library of information for possible future use. The drawings clearly show his excitement in recording the very different scenery, architecture, antiqui-ties and customs of the country, but it was the brilliant Italian light that made the most impact on him. He produced some exquisite watercolours of Como, Venice and Naples, and some bolder colour studies made in Rome, responding to the warmth and light of the Mediterranean atmosphere. The new vision suggested to Turner by his visit to Italy in 1819, which Lawrence had foreseen, matured in subsequent years; its effects will be apparent in the next exhibition in this continuing series.

3 **Porch of St George's, Bloomsbury** *c.*1810

18 **View from Richmond Hill** *c.*1815

11 **Ivy Bridge** *c*.1813

12 **Hulks on the Tamar: Twilight** *c*.1813

13 **On the Plym Estuary, near Crabtree** 1813

19 **Loss of a Man o'War** c.1817

24 **Richmond, Yorkshire** *c*.1818

25 **Gordale Scar** *c*.1816

29 **Boppart; Colour Study** *?c.*1820

31 **Tivoli; Colour Study** *c.*1817

38 **Rome: The Claudian Aqueduct** 1819

28 **The Battle of Fort Rock, Val d' Aosta,
Piedmont, 1796** 1815

33 **Venice: Looking East from the Guidecca** 1819

36 **View over the Roman Campagna** 1819

46 **Naples, the Castel dell'Ovo** 1819

44 **Tivoli, with the Cascades** 1819

[20]

Catalogue

All measurements are given in millimetres, height before width. Works illustrated in colour are marked*

Abbreviations

B&J   Butlin, Martin and Evelyn Joll, *The Paintings of J.M.W. Turner*, 2 vols., 1984 (revised edition)

R.   Rawlinson, W.G., *The Engraved Work of J.M.W. Turner, R.A.*, 2 vols., 1908–13

R.L.   Rawlinson, W.G., *Turner's Liber Studiorum*, 1878 (1st edition)

T B   Finberg, A.J., *A Complete Inventory of the Drawings of the Turner Bequest*, 2 vols., 1909

W.   Wilton, A., *The Life and Work of J.M.W. Turner*, 1979

For other published material which is abbreviated in the text, see Bibliography.

1 **Interior of the Great Room, Somerset House** *c.*1810
Pencil and watercolour
669 × 1000 ($26\frac{5}{16} \times 39\frac{3}{8}$)
Turner Bequest; CXCV 70
D17040

Turner had been appointed to the post of Professor of Perspective at the Royal Academy in 1807 but it was not until 1811 that he gave his first lecture. Although the lectures were poorly delivered, they were well-researched and were illustrated by a series of large drawings.

The Great Room in Somerset House, where the Royal Academy was then housed, was that in which the Academy exhibitions were held and where Turner delivered his lectures. He has chosen here to show a view of the room itself, looking up at the ceiling, as one of his illustrations. It was presumably used for a discussion on geometrical forms, for a critic complained of Turner's poor grammar, stating that he 'talked of "elliptical circles", called the semi-elliptical windows of the lecture room semi-circular, and so forth…' (*New Monthly Magazine*, 1 Feb. 1816)

2 **Two Views of the Monument** *c.*1810
Pencil and watercolour
675×1011 $(26\frac{9}{16} \times 39\frac{5}{8})$
Turner Bequest; CXCV 151
D17122

The perspective drawings include several beautiful architectural studies in watercolour along with more diagrammatic examples. They are believed to have been prepared in the year or so before his first lecture in 1811 and seem to form a homogeneous group since they all use the same limited range of colours and are executed in a similar style. However, Turner was continually changing the content of his lectures from one course to the next and there is therefore no reason why he should not have similarly continued to alter the diagrams; new drawings were perhaps executed up until 1828 when his lecture courses ceased.

Several of the diagrams, such as these illustrations of Wren's Monument to the Great Fire of London, are of architectural features seen in perspective and are concerned with the way in which details can become distorted when seen from below (see cat.no.3).

3 **Porch of St George's, Bloomsbury*** *c.*1810
Pen and ink and watercolour
708×348 $(27\frac{7}{8} \times 13\frac{11}{16})$
Turner Bequest; CXCV 144
D17115

Turner used two diagrams of St George's, Bloomsbury as illustrations for a perspective lecture. This view, showing a straightfoward elevation of the building, was contrasted with another (TB CXCV 145) showing the spire as seen at a steep angle from below (see cat.no.47). The illustrations were intended to demonstrate the way in which the eye foreshortens the tower and 'bends' the straight lines of the spire, as well as how the statue of George II on the top of the spire was designed to be seen from a distance and at an angle.

Turner used examples of other modern buildings including the Brocklesby Mausoleum (TB CXCV 130) and Pulteney Bridge, Bath (TB CXCV 114) as illustrations for the lectures.

along the Thames), the group of oil sketches made in Devon have a more personal feel to them and appear to share a similar purpose in recording the topography of the countryside around Plymouth, as do the watercolours he was making at the same time. Their warm, rich colours and picturesque compositions convey, with a vivid immediacy, Turner's love of the tranquil Devon scenery.

14 Shaugh Bridge, near Plymouth 1813
    Oil on prepared paper
    158 × 266 ($6\frac{3}{16}$ × $10\frac{7}{16}$)
    Turner Bequest; CXXX I
    D09215

The Devonshire oil sketches are often thought to have been executed out of doors, a practice which Turner used on very few occasions. Charles Lock Eastlake records that the Plymouth landscape painter, Ambrose Bowden Johns, prepared a box of oil colours for Turner who 'made his oil sketches freely in our presence' (Thornbury, 1862, I, p.220). On the other hand, Cyrus Redding describes a picnic on Mount Edgcumbe when 'Turner showed the ladies some of his sketches in oil which he had brought with him, perhaps to verify them' (Redding, 1852, p.155), which would imply that they had been executed away from the motif. Whether or not Turner actually painted these oil sketches in the presence of his friends or was simply prepared to show his work, the artist's usual reticence seems to have been forgotten on this tour.

15 The Plym Estuary from Boringdon Park 1813
    Oil on prepared paper
    245 × 305 ($9\frac{5}{8}$ × 12)
    Turner Bequest; CXXX Æ
    D09211

Fifteen oil sketches made by Turner in the neighbourhood of Plymouth are known to exist, although many more were probably executed which have since deteriorated or remain untraced (see Smiles, 1989). They are nearly all on small sheets of paper of roughly the same size. They are painted in rich, earthy colours and are of an unusual directness. This sketch, however, is nearly twice the size of the others and is more detailed, including figures and animals and the fort on the hill.

Turner executed a series of full-scale oil paintings as a result of his West country tours; among them are 'Ivy Bridge Mill, Devonshire' (B&J 122), 'Hulks on the Tamar' (B&J 119), 'St Mawes at the Pilchard Season' (B&J 123; Tate Gallery) and 'Crossing the Brook' (B&J 130; Tate Gallery). The purpose of these small oil sketches is unclear; they do not seem to have been seen as preparatory sketches for larger oils but no doubt the information gleaned during their execution was valuable in Turner's work on the finished pictures as well as the series of watercolours for the engraver.

16 **Hurstmonceux Castle** *c.*1816
   Pencil
   200×311 $(8\frac{7}{8} \times 12\frac{1}{4})$
   Turner Bequest; CXXXVIII 5
   D10324

Turner made several pencil sketches like this one in preparation for a series of finished watercolours for the Sussex M.P., Jack Fuller. This is a page from the *Views in Sussex* sketchbook which he used, along with the *Vale of Heathfield* sketchbook (cat.no.50) and others, while simultaneously collecting material for the *Southern Coast* series (see cat.no.10).

   This meticulous drawing was closely copied in the finished watercolour (cat.no.17), particularly in the architectural details of Hurstmonceux Castle and the immediate surrounding landscape. The foreground of the composition, however, is not worked out as carefully and Turner has inscribed 'Cattle' and '8' where a group of four cows appear in the watercolour.

17 **Hurstmonceux Castle, Sussex** 1817
   Watercolour
   381×559 (15×22)
   Private Collection

In about 1810 Turner was commissioned to execute a series of watercolours for Jack Fuller, of his home, Rosehill in East Sussex, and the surrounding countryside. The commission may have been given when Turner visited Rosehill to begin work on an oil painting of the house early in that year (B&J 211; see Farington Diary 21 April 1810); but the thirteen watercolours do not appear to have been executed until around 1815 or 1816. Eight finished watercolours (all but one of which belonged to Fuller; W.430) were engraved between 1816 and 1820 for Cooke's *Views in Sussex* and four other watercolours of the group appeared as coloured aquatints in about 1818 (R.822–5).

   Two parts of *Views in Sussex* had been advertised and six plates were published in the first part but the second, to be called *Views in Hastings and its Vicinity* did not appear, owing to a quarrel between Cooke and the publisher, John Murray. The plate of Hurstmonceux, for which this watercolour was the basis, was begun as an open etching in 1820 (R.135) but was never completed or published.

18 **View from Richmond Hill*** *c.*1815
Pencil and watercolour
188 × 272 ($7\frac{3}{8}$ × $10\frac{11}{16}$)
Turner Bequest; CXCVII B
D17192

This stretch of the Thames, as seen from Richmond
Hill, was an area much loved by Turner, who lived for
several years in the vicinity of Richmond: he built his
own villa, Sandycombe Lodge, at Twickenham (see
cat.no.49).

It was a view that Turner was to draw many times; an
unfinished watercolour study of it was sketched as early
as 1795 (TB XXVII K) and two finished watercolours
were engraved in later years (w.518 and 879). His most
magnificent statement of the theme is the large picture he
painted a few years after this unassuming study, in
1819; 'England: Richmond Hill on the Prince Regent's
Birthday' (B&J 140; Tate Gallery).

19 **Loss of a Man o' War*** *c.*1817
Pencil, watercolour and bodycolour
311 × 460 ($12\frac{1}{4}$ × $18\frac{1}{8}$)
Turner Bequest; CXCVI N
D17178

Turner visited Yorkshire virtually annually throughout
the 1810s, primarily to stay with his friend and patron
Walter Fawkes at Farnley Hall, near Leeds. Fawkes
had collected Turner's work for several years previously
but it was during these years that his patronage
flourished, extending to over 200 watercolours and six
oils, at a cost of around £3,500. Many of these works
were specifically commissioned by Fawkes, such as the
series of views of the house and surrounding countryside, the album of bird drawings and the 'Fairfaxiana',
a series of watercolours based on Fawkes's Civil War
collection.

This sheet is a colour study for a finished watercolour
of *c.* 1818 (w.500), one of several marine watercolours
by Turner which Fawkes acquired. The final version
may have been intended as a companion to 'A First-
Rate taking in stores' (w.499), whose execution is
vividly described in a recollection by Edith Mary
Fawkes (see typescript, National Gallery Library, London, quoted Wilton, 1987, p.114), which throws considerable light on Turner's working methods at this
time.

The study is inscribed 'Begun [or 'Beginning'] for
Dear Fawkes of Farnley', testimony to the close friend-
ship between the two men. The inscription was perhaps
added after Fawkes's death in 1825.

20 **The Vale of Pickering with Huntsmen** ?c.1815
Pencil and watercolour
192 × 244 (7⁹⁄₁₆ × 9⅝)
Turner Bequest; CXXI Q
D08273

While staying with Fawkes, Turner explored the surrounding countryside of Wharfedale and the Washburn Valley in order to execute the series of bodycolour landscapes which Fawkes referred to as 'the Wharfedales'. However, he also travelled further afield in the county, to the dales and to the coast, often to collect material for engraving commissions (see cat.no.22).

This watercolour, thought to represent the Vale of Pickering, north of Farnley, bears similarities with the 'Wharfedale' series and other finished views of Yorkshire of this period, both in its expansive topography and depiction of a sporting scene (see, for instance, 'Shooting party on Hawksworth Moor'; w.610; or 'Grouse Shooting'; w.535); it may well have been executed at around the same time. In this watercolour, Turner has included the humorous detail of an unseated huntsman calling after his horse.

21 **Kirkstall Abbey** c.1816
Pencil and watercolour
187 × 238 (7⅞ × 9⅜)
Turner Bequest; CLV 19
D12260

The ruins of Kirkstall Abbey, near Leeds, were drawn several times by Turner, from his earliest tour to Yorkshire in 1797. This sketch is a page from the *Kirkstall Lock* sketchbook which he probably used while staying at Farnley. No finished watercolours of the Lock or the ruined Abbey were made during this period, although two finished subjects were executed for the 'Rivers of England' series in the mid 1820s ('Kirkstall Abbey'; w.741 and 'Kirkstall Lock'; w.745).

22 **Kirkby Lonsdale: Colour Study** c.1817
Pencil, watercolour and bodycolour
387 × 485 (15¼ × 19⅛)
Turner Bequest; CXCVI V
D17186

Turner embarked on several engraving commissions for topographical views in the North of England during this period, no doubt undertaken on account of his frequent visits to Yorkshire when staying at Farnley. These engraving projects included *Leodis and Elmete* and Surtees's *History of Durham* (see cat.no.26), as well as the *History of Richmondshire*. The *Richmondshire* series was commissioned by Dr. Thomas Dunham Whitaker in about 1816, as part of a projected *History of Yorkshire*, and proved to be one of the most important series for the engraver that Turner executed.

Turner embarked on a tour of the North of England in 1816, in order to sketch the places selected as subjects for Whitaker's plates. Prior to this series of water-colours, Turner had intermittently made preparatory studies or 'beginnings' in broad colour washes in order to establish the main tonal areas of the composition. But it was during the course of this project that he seems to have adopted the practise on a more regular basis.

This is one of two colour studies of the Lune Valley seen from Kirby Lonsdale churchyard (see also TB CXCVI W). Like other colour studies which Turner made, it focuses on the main format of the composition rather than local incident; by a comparison with the finished view which was engraved for the *History of Richmondshire*, (cat.no.23), this study lacks the fore-ground trees, buildings and figures in the churchyard, although the distant view is followed very closely.

CHARLES HEATH AFTER J.M.W. TURNER

23 **Kirby [sic] Lonsdale** 1822
   Engraving
   $195 \times 278 \ (7\frac{5}{8} \times 10\frac{15}{16})$
   T04475

Turner eventually produced twenty elaborate water-colours for the *History of Richmondshire* which were engraved between 1818 and 1823. The project was never completed, perhaps due to Whitaker's untimely death in 1821.

The finished watercolour on which this engraving was based was executed *c.*1818 (W.578). Turner has developed the composition from its earlier stage (cat.no.22) by the inclusion of the churchyard in which a group of schoolboys are aiming missiles at a pile of books. It was a view chosen by Whitaker perhaps in response to Wordsworth's recommendation; 'by no means omit looking at the Vale of Lune from the Churchyard' (*Guide to the Lakes*, 1810).

24 **Richmond, Yorkshire*** *c.*1818
   Pencil, watercolour and bodycolour
   $391 \times 485 \ (15\frac{3}{8} \times 19\frac{1}{8})$
   Turner Bequest; CXCVII H
   D17198

Turner's tour of the North of England in 1816 was extremely arduous, and undertaken in poor weather conditions. Nevertheless, he gathered a vast store of sketches, filling three sketchbooks, which he used in executing the subsequent colour studies and finished watercolours.

This study of Richmond, however, does not appear to be based on pencil sketches, although it does show the same view, looking towards the High Bridge from upstream, which Turner depicted after his first visit to Richmond in 1797 (TB XXXVI V). It did not form the basis of a finished watercolour in the *Richmondshire* series, although it is similar to many of the colour studies for the project. Two other watercolours of Richmond, showing different views of the town and castle, were engraved (R.169 and 170).

25 **Gordale Scar*** *c.*1816
Pencil and oil on paper
549×767 $(21\frac{5}{8} \times 30\frac{3}{16})$
Turner Bequest; CLIV O
D12113

Gordale Scar may have been intended as a *Richmondshire* subject, though no view of it was completed. It is a dramatic natural phenomenon, similar to other subjects in the series such as 'High Force' and 'Hardraw Falls'. Turner must have visited the gorge on the outset of the tour he made in connection with the *Richmondshire* project, since Fawkes's wife recorded in her diary; 'Thurs 25 [July 1816]. Went to see Gordale Waterfall. Returned Home. Heavy rain. Turner went on a sketching tour.' However, this study is much larger than others for the series and is executed in an unusual variety of media, including oil paint, with gum or varnish. It may have been intended as the subject for a painting, perhaps one to rival James Ward's huge canvas of the scene of 1814 (Tate Gallery).

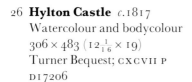

26 **Hylton Castle** *c.*1817
Watercolour and bodycolour
306×483 $(12\frac{1}{16} \times 19)$
Turner Bequest; CXCVII P
D17206

As well as the *Richmondshire* series of views, Turner was also commissioned to make designs to be engraved for Robert Surtees's *History of Durham*. In the autumn of 1817, while he was based at Raby Castle in Durham (see cat.no.52), Turner made a tour of the surrounding countryside, collecting material for this project. Three views were engraved for the series by Samuel Rawle; Gibside, Co. Durham (R.142), Raby Castle (R.143) and Hylton Castle, Durham (R.141) for which this is a preparatory colour study. An initial sketch of this view can be found in the *Raby* sketchbook (TB CLVI 10).

27 Durham Cathedral with a Rainbow *c.*1817

Pencil and watercolour

550 × 369 (21⅝ × 14½)

Turner Bequest; CCLXIII 125

D25247

Turner had visited Durham early in his career, in 1797, and had made several drawings of the Cathedral, including a striking large interior (TB XXXVI G). Another watercolour study of Durham with a rainbow is in the *Helmsley* sketchbook of 1801 (TB LIII 98). The present view was probably executed in around 1817 when Turner visited the city while collecting material for the *History of Durham* (see cat.no.26); there are several sketches of the Cathedral seen across the river in the *Durham N. Shore* sketchbook which he used on that tour (TB CLVII 6–12). This study is similar in its bold areas of strong colour to those made for the *Richmondshire* and *Durham* projects such as 'Kirkby Lonsdale' (cat.no.22) and 'Hylton Castle' (cat.no.26).

Turner has written the title and the words 'Willow paper' on this drawing. This is probably the name of the maker or mill where the paper was made, since the paper does not seem to have been made from willow bark. The sheet was originally half of a larger one; the other part, 'Storm over a Rocky Coast' (TB CCLXIII 32), has also been inscribed 'Willow paper', indicating that Turner himself must have divided the sheet into two.

28 The Battle of Fort Rock, Val d'Aosta, Piedmont, 1796* 1815

Watercolour and bodycolour

696 × 1015 (27⅜ × 39¹⁵⁄₁₆)

Turner Bequest; LXXX G

D04900

This magnificent watercolour was exhibited at the Royal Academy in 1815, accompanied by ten lines from Turner's manuscript poem, the 'Fallacies of Hope'. It is one of the few finished watercolours that Turner made for exhibition during this decade and he must therefore have attached considerable importance to it. It is the most ambitious of a series of large finished watercolours of alpine subjects that he made after his tour of Switzerland in 1802. The composition was originally drawn in the *St Gothard and Mont Blanc* sketchbook (w.360) that formed the basis of a finished watercolour of *c.*1804 in which a group of country girls admire the scenery (w.369); the view of the Val d'Aosta shown here is used as the setting for a dramatic history-piece.

The watercolour represents an incident during Napoleon's invasion of Italy in 1796 and contrasts the violent struggle of the armies and the awesome scenery of the mountain gorge with the poignant foreground group of a mother and child tending a wounded soldier. It is one of Turner's most accomplished achievements in watercolour with its exquisite rendering of the jagged rocks, glimpsed in sunshine through clouds and billowing smoke, above the tenebrous ravine.

It was not sold at the Academy exhibition and 'was found after Turner's death, blocking up a window in an out-house, placed there no doubt to save window tax' (*Ruskin on Pictures*, 1902, p.421).

29 **Boppart; Colour Study*** *?c.*1820
  Pencil and watercolour
  186×295 ($7\frac{5}{16} \times 11\frac{5}{8}$)
  Turner Bequest; CCLXIII 259
  D25382

In the late summer of 1817, Turner made his first tour to the continent since peace had been made in Europe, visiting the battlefield of Waterloo, travelling up the Rhine as far as Mainz and returning through Holland. As well as making numerous pencil drawings in four sketchbooks (see cat.no.53), Turner executed a series of bodycolour sketches which were all acquired by Fawkes (w.636–686). These drawings, probably made at Farnley on his return, vary considerably in their degree of finish; many have the appearance of quick sketches, perhaps made on the spot, while others are more detailed. Around 1820, some of the subjects were worked into finished watercolours such as those for Sir John Swinburne or his son; the patron's choice of views was probably made from the drawings in Fawkes's collection. Other subjects were worked up with the intention of being engraved for a proposed series of Rhine views to be published by Cooke, a project which was subsequently abandoned (w.687–9a).

This colour study relates to the view of Boppart (w.652) which was one of the group of Rhine drawings acquired by Fawkes, but for which it seems unlikely to have been a preparatory study; the Rhine drawings seem too spontaneous and intimate in feel to have warranted preparatory drawings and, indeed, there do not appear to be any for other subjects in the group. The sheet is more likely to be a colour study for one of the 'duplicate' Rhine views made in around 1820 for the Swinburnes or another patron, or alternatively for the Cooke project.

30 Sooneck with Bacharach in the distance

?c.1820
Pencil and watercolour
$402 \times 564 \ (15\frac{13}{16} \times 22\frac{3}{16})$
Turner Bequest; CCLXIII 182
D25304

A view of Sooneck formed one of the series of Rhine drawings acquired by Fawkes in 1817 (w.671) and a larger, more finished version of the subject was completed in around 1820 (w.693). This watercolour is likely to have been made prior to the finshed view (see under cat.no.29). Unusually, another very similar, although smaller, colour study exists for this subject (TB CCLXIII 120), which cannot have been a study for the 1817 view since it is watermarked 1819. It seems that Turner was particularly attracted to the broad sweep of the river and the grandeur of the cliffs in this view and was perhaps intending to make more than one completed version of the subject.

31 Tivoli; Colour Study* c.1817

Pencil and watercolour
$667 \times 1006 \ (26\frac{1}{4} \times 39\frac{5}{8})$
Turner Bequest; CXCVII A
D17191

Although in the early nineteenth century Italy was still regarded as the Mecca for all practising artists, Turner did not have the opportunity of going to Italy until 1819, at the age of forty-four. This did not prevent him from drawing Italian subjects prior to his journey. He completed a series of eighteen watercolours, based on camera-lucida pencil outlines by James Hakewill, for Hakewill's *Picturesque Tour in Italy*, published in engraved form between 1818 and 1820. In 1817, two large finished watercolours of Italian subjects were completed; 'Eruption of Vesuvius' (w.697) and 'Landscape: Composition of Tivoli' (w.495).

This is a preparatory colour study for the latter. It is close to the finished watercolour both in size and in its composition, although the Temple of the Sibyl, so prominent in the final version, does not appear in this study. It is interesting to compare Turner's vision of Tivoli based on a Claudian ideal, for which his ideas were worked out here, with the watercolours that he made when he visited Tivoli two years later (cat.no.44). The strong colours, such as the dark greens and ochres in this study, are used in a purely formal way to be adapted more subtly in the finished version; they are very different from the muted greys and greens in his naturalistic studies of 1819.

32 **On Lake Como** 1819
Watercolour
224×290 ($8\frac{13}{16} \times 11\frac{7}{16}$)
Turner Bequest; CLXXXI 1
D15251

Turner set out for Italy in July 1819, well prepared for the tour with notes and guide-books and with a strenuous itinerary planned. He produced a phenomenal number of drawings and watercolours in Italy, collected in nineteen sketchbooks, before his return to England in January 1820. Some of these books, particularly those containing coloured sketches in watercolour or bodycolour, have since been broken up.

This view of Lake Como, for instance, was drawn in the *Como and Venice* sketchbook; along with a similar view without the foreground boats (TB CLXXXI 2), it is the first of the watercolours Turner executed in Italy. The delicacy and subtlety of the colours with their evocation of warm light are evidence of the freshness of his approach to the new landscape.

33 **Venice: Looking East from the Guidecca*** 1819
Watercolour
223×287 ($8\frac{3}{4} \times 11\frac{1}{4}$)
Turner Bequest; CLXXXI 5
D15255

Although Turner made numerous pencil drawings of Venice during his brief visit in September 1819, he executed only four watercolours of the city (see also cat.nos.34 and 35). These views are exceptional in their luminosity and carefully controlled use of delicate watercolour washes. In this study, primary colours are used in an unusually direct and economical way which nevertheless evokes the detailed skyline of the city and activity of the gondolas in the foreground.

The actual viewpoint Turner has taken is difficult to ascertain; it may be that this was primarily a study of the sky, to which Turner added an idealised view of the city skyline. It is interesting to compare it with other studies of cloud effects in the *Skies* sketchbook (cat.no.57).

34 Venice: S. Giorgio Maggiore 1819
Watercolour
223 × 287 (8¾ × 11¼)
Turner Bequest; CLXXXI 4
D15254

The Venetian watercolours made in the *Como and Venice* sketchbook are particularly innovative in their experiments with atmospheric effects, capturing both the quality of the bright Italian light and a sense of the time of day in which they were executed. This striking watercolour, composed in subtle shades of green wash which suggest the shadows on the buildings, gives a sense of the early morning sun rising upon the city.

35 Venice: Campanile and Ducal Palace 1819
Pencil and watercolour
225 × 289 (8⅞ × 11⅜)
Turner Bequest; CLXXXI 7
D15258

Compared with the other Venetian watercolours, this view, with its focus on a group of prominent buildings, is much bolder in its approach and was perhaps drawn with a different purpose in mind. The Campanile of St Mark's and the Doge's Palace are seen frontally from the Bacino and are rendered in a warm beige which is contrasted with the unmodulated blue washes of the sky and water. As a study, it was perhaps the most useful drawing that Turner made during this visit to Venice and was apparently incorporated in his first oil painting of the city of 1833, 'Bridge of Sighs, Ducal Palace and Custom-House, Venice: Canaletti painting' (B&J 349; Tate Gallery).

36 View over the Roman Campagna* 1819
Watercolour
254 × 401 (10 × 15¾)
Turner Bequest; CLXXXVII 34
D16122

Turner arrived in Rome in October 1819 where he worked to a strict schedule of travelling and sketching. As well as the hundreds of drawings of antiquities and buildings of Rome, he also made numerous studies of the open Campagna around the city. This watercolour, from the *Naples, Rome C. Studies* sketchbook, showing a stretch of the Campagna with the Ponte Salario, shares the same freshness as the Como and Venice views with its response to the colour and light of the landscape. Turner used three sketchbooks during his stay in Rome which included the letter 'C' in his title; the other two

sketchbooks are *Rome C. Studies* (see cat.nos.37–43) and *Small Roman C. Studies* (cat.no.56). The 'C' is often thought to stand for 'colour' since the books all contain coloured sketches, but it may alternatively indicate 'Composition', since they perhaps include subjects intended for further development.

37 **Rome: Arches of Constantine and Titus** 1819
Pencil, watercolour and bodycolour on white
paper prepared with a grey wash
228 × 369 (9 × 14½)
Turner Bequest; CLXXXIX 40
D16367

As well as the watercolour views of the Italian landscape which exquisitely express the impact that the Mediterranean light must have had on him when he experienced it for the first time, Turner also executed several colour studies in bodycolour on grey toned paper. These strong colours tend to evoke the warmth and heaviness of the atmosphere rather than the brightness and clarity of the light which watercolour on white paper captured so well. The monumentality of the ancient buildings in Rome, such as the triumphal arches in the Forum shown here, are rendered with more solidity and force by Turner's choice of technique.

Since the seventeenth century, the Roman Forum had been popular with artists such as Claude Lorraine, Richard Wilson and Piranesi, whom Turner greatly admired. Their work obviously inspired him for he sketched the overgrown site from every conceivable angle. Turner seems to have been attracted to the way in which the trees and local peasants provided a pastoral setting for the ancient ruins, for he often included figures going about their daily activities, such as the one driving his cattle and poultry in this drawing.

38 **Rome: The Claudian Aqueduct*** 1819
Watercolour and bodycolour on white paper
prepared with a grey wash
229 × 369 (9 × 14½)
Turner Bequest; CLXXXIX 36
D16363

The hoard of notes which Turner accumulated in his sketchbooks while in Rome testify to his almost obsessive desire to record as much as he could of the landscape and architecture of the city for possible future use. Of the colour studies that he made, such as those in the *Rome C. Studies* sketchbook, he seems to have been particularly interested in the architecture of Ancient

Rome, rather than the palaces or churches built during the Renaissance.

Although the ancient monuments of the Claudian Aqueduct and 'Temple of Minerva Medica', depicted here were obvious attractions to the Romantic tourist, Turner has depicted them in a somewhat cursory way, concentrating rather on the surrounding landscape and dramatic sunset.

39 **Rome from the Baths of Caracalla** 1819
Pencil and watercolour on white paper prepared with a grey wash
228 × 369 (9 × 14½)
Turner Bequest; CLXXXIX 8
D16334

Turner made more colour studies in Rome than in any other Italian city. This expansive view combines detailed observation with broad atmospheric effects and, like many similar subjects, it is only partially worked up in colour.

It is not clear if any of the coloured drawings made in Italy were executed directly from the motif, but this would seem unlikely for Turner commented that 'it would take up too much time to colour in the open air. He could make 15 or 16 pencil sketches to one coloured' (Finberg 1961, p. 262). It is possible that some of the watercolours, perhaps those in Venice, Naples or the Roman Campagna, were executed out of doors; but the more detailed effects of the studies in bodycolour were worked up in his studio.

40 **View of Rome from the Janiculum** 1819
Pencil on white paper prepared with a grey wash
229 × 367 (9 × 14⁷⁄₁₆)
Turner Bequest; CLXXXIX 12
D16338

Many of the drawings in Rome which Turner made on paper prepared with a grey wash ground were pencil studies, either of particular buildings such as the Colosseum (cat.no.42), or of panoramic views of the city seen from one of the surrounding hills. This view of Rome from the Janiculum, with Palazzo Corsini in the left foreground, is typical of these studies; the grey wash has been rubbed and scratched out in parts to create a variety of tone which is combined with highly detailed pencil work.

41 **Rome from the Vatican** 1819
Pencil, pen and brown ink, with bodycolour on
white paper prepared with a grey wash
(discoloured)
233×371 $(9\frac{3}{16} \times 14\frac{5}{8})$
Turner Bequest; CLXXXIX 41
D16368

Despite the mass of reference material collected on the
1819 tour of Italy, Turner made only one finished oil
painting of an Italian subject immediately after his
return to England in 1820, 'Rome from the Vatican:
Raffaelle, accompanied by La Fornarina, preparing his
Pictures for the Decoration of the Loggia' (B&J 228;
Tate Gallery). This drawing is a preparatory study for
the painting and, unlike the other studies that he made
in Rome on grey paper, it is executed in pen and ink
with highlights added in lead white; Turner had
obviously conceived the idea of using this composition
for a more elaborate work at an early stage.

The panoramic view of Rome and distant Appenine
mountains seen through the arcaded loggia of the
Vatican palace seems to sum up Turner's reactions to
Italy; it encompasses in one grand vision all the
elements of the country's architecture, landscape and
civilisation that he had studied so carefully.

42 **Rome: The Colosseum** 1819
Pencil on white paper prepared with a grey wash
232×368 $(9\frac{1}{8} \times 14\frac{1}{2})$
Turner Bequest; CLXXXIX 23
D16349

Although no finished watercolours were executed during Turner's visit to Italy, seven more detailed Italian
subjects were completed shortly after his return in 1820.
They were all acquired by Walter Fawkes. This view of
the Colosseum, with a flock of goats in the foreground,
was used as the basis for a finished watercolour of the
subject (W.723), now in the British Museum. The
watercolour, however, shows the building from a lower
viewpoint and with the figures and animals reduced in
scale in order to increase the dramatic effect of the
composition.

43 **St Peter's from the Villa Barberini** 1819
Pencil, watercolour and bodycolour on white paper
prepared with a grey wash
231 × 372 ($9\frac{1}{16}$ × $14\frac{5}{8}$)
Turner Bequest; CLXXXIX 21
D16347

This view of St Peter's is closely based on a detailed
pencil drawing in the same sketchbook (TB CLXXXIX 7)
which would probably have been made on the spot.
Both views are executed on the grey toned paper Turner
used in Rome when working on a larger scale; he
returned to using watercolour on white paper when he
travelled south to Naples after his departure from
Rome.

44 **Tivoli, with the Cascades*** 1819
Pencil and watercolour
252 × 404 ($9\frac{7}{8}$ × $15\frac{7}{8}$)
Turner Bequest; CLXXXVII 32
D16120

The cliffs, cascades, towers and temples of Tivoli made
it an inspiring subject for landscape painters. Indeed,
Turner had chosen to illustrate Tivoli in 1817 before he
had seen it for himself (see cat.no.31), having acquired a
familiarity with the setting from the work of other
artists, most notably, Claude. Turner's enthusiasm for
the place at first hand is demonstrated by the numerous
pencil sketches which he made in the *Tivoli and Rome*
and *Tivoli* sketchbooks (TB CLXXIX and CLXXXIII) as
well as two watercolour views in the *Naples, Rome C.
Studies* sketchbook, of which this is one.

This broadly handled watercolour study concen-
trates on the varying shades of greens and greys of the
dramatic landscape bathed in brilliant light; in the
other view (TB CLXXXVII 28) the buildings are more
carefully observed.

45 **Naples** 1819
Pencil
255 × 403 (10 × $15\frac{7}{8}$)
Turner Bequest; CLXXXVII 4
D16091

Although many of the larger pencil drawings made in
Rome were executed on grey toned paper, Turner used
unprepared white paper while working in Naples. This
view of the buildings along the Bay of Naples and the
rising cliffs behind them is typical of the meticulous
observation demonstrated in all his pencil drawings
during the Italian tour.

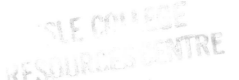

46 **Naples, the Castel dell'Ovo*** 1819
Pencil and watercolour
255 × 404 (10 × 15⅞)
Turner Bequest; CLXXXVII 6
D16093

Turner apparently went to Naples from Rome to witness an eruption of Vesuvius; other watercolours which he made there show the active volcano. One of these (TB CLXXXVII 13) was worked up as a finished watercolour for Walter Fawkes, 'Bay of Naples, the view from Capodimonte' (W.722). The watercolour views made in Naples and Tivoli (cat.no.43) share the same freshness as the Venetian watercolours, perhaps because they are also executed on white paper. This delicate colour study is one of a group of panoramic views looking out from Naples across the bay to Capri, with the Castel dell'Ovo in the foreground.

Windmill and Lock sketchbook c.1810
47 **St George's, Bloomsbury**
Pencil and pen and ink
87 × 226 (3⅜ × 8⅞)
Turner Bequest; CXIV 65 verso, 66
D08045, D08046

The copious notes in his sketchbooks, and the numerous manuscript drafts (now in the British Library, Department of Manuscripts, Add. 46151) testify to Turner's assiduous researches into the subject of perspective for his lectures to the Academy Schools. His notes here refer to Trajan's Column, which he also used (like St George's, Bloomsbury) as an illustration to demonstrate the appearance of a building from various viewpoints. This sketch shows the spire of St George's as seen from below. The composition was used for a large watercolour study displayed during one of the lectures (see cat.no.3).

This book also contains several other sketches of St George's and further subjects used in the perspective lectures, as well as designs for Sandycombe Lodge (see cat.no.49).

Devonshire Coast No. 1 sketchbook 1811
48 **Ivy Bridge?**
Pencil
115 × 144 (4½ × 5⅝)
Turner Bequest; CXXIII 153 verso, 154
D08655, D08656

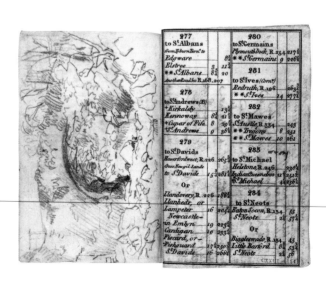

Turner took this copy of the *British Itinerary*, a traveller's guide-book, with him on his first Devonshire tour of 1811. He used the interleaving pages to make a large number of pencil sketches of the scenery, including this view of a rocky stream under a bridge. It possibly shows Ivy Bridge (see cat.no.11).

The book also contains Turner's longest poem which he had written en route and perhaps hoped to adapt as an accompanying text to the *Southern Coast* engravings. The poem, which covers many topics relating to the sea and includes patriotic passages concerning English history, was, however, not incorporated into the prose descriptions by the journalist, William Coombe, which were chosen to be published alongside the engravings.

Woodcock Shooting sketchbook *c.*1811

49 **Study for 'Crossing The Brook'? and Designs for Sandycombe Lodge**
Pen and ink and pencil
110 × 356 (4 5/16 × 14)
Turner Bequest; CXXIX 51 verso, 52
D09128, D09129

Turner's work as an architect came to the fore in the period 1810–20. Not only did he make plans to rebuild his London Gallery in Queen Anne Street and design the East Lodge Gates at Farnley Hall, but he also designed and superintended the building of his own villa, Sandycombe Lodge, at Twickenham. The pencil sketches shown here are plans for the house which was built between 1812–13; Turner lived there until 1826.

On the opposite page of this sketchbook is a pen and ink study for a classical picture. The composition is close to the oil paintings of 'Mercury and Herse', 1811 and 'Crossing the Brook', 1815. Since this sketchbook was probably used around the time of Turner's first visit to Devon in 1811, it may well be that this drawing, and others like it in the book, are studies for a painting inspired by the Devonshire countryside; 'Crossing the Brook' was the only such subject to be realised.

Vale of Heathfield sketchbook *c.*1816

50 **Vale of Ashburnham**
Pencil
181 × 456 (7 1/8 × 17 15/16)
Turner Bequest; CXXXVII 68 verso, 69
D10312, D10313

This drawing formed the basis for the finished water-colour of *The Vale of Ashburnham* W.425; British Museum), which was engraved for the *Views in Sussex* in 1817 (R.131). Like the sketch of Hurstmonceux (cat.no.16), the view corresponds very closely to Turner's final version; from its earliest conception, he has included both the bullock-cart and the distinctive grouping of trees on the right. Turner made another view of Ashburnham, looking inland, for Fuller, which was aquatinted by J. C. Stadler in about 1818 (R.823).

Farnley sketchbook *c.*1816

51 **The Library, Farnley Hall**
Pencil
111 × 370 ($4\frac{3}{8}$ × $14\frac{9}{16}$)
Turner Bequest; CLIII 15 verso, 16
DI2021, DI2022

The Farnley sketchbook contains several detailed pencil drawings of Farnley Hall, including views of the exterior of the house and grounds, such as the Lodge Gates designed by Turner (see cat.no.49) as well as interiors, such as this. These sketches were used for a number of the finished drawings executed for Fawkes in about 1818 (see cat.nos.19 and 20).

This sketch, which is continued to the right on p.17, depicts the elegant Library in the new part of the house, added in 1790 by John Carr of York. This interior was not developed as a finished watercolour although two finished drawings of the old Library at Farnley were executed (W.595 and 566). However, it must have been intended for use in a more substantial view, for Turner has made annotations such as '27' and '25', recording the number of times the decorative ceiling motifs are repeated, as well as making a note of the colours, inscribing areas 'red' and 'black'.

Raby sketchbook 1817

52 **Raby Castle**
Pencil and watercolour
232 × 656 ($9\frac{1}{8}$ × $25\frac{13}{16}$)
Turner Bequest; CLVI 23 verso, 24
DI2300, DI2301

Turner went straight to Raby after his return from the Rhine in 1817 (see cat.no.29). He used this large sketchbook to collect relevant material for an oil painting of 'Raby Castle, the Seat of the Earl of Darlington' (B&J 136) which he exhibited at the Royal Academy in 1818.

This is one of numerous studies of the castle, some showing closer views concentrating on the architectural features, as well as others, such as this, of the castle set in a panoramic sweep of countryside. It is the only one, however, to have been partially worked up in colour, perhaps in order to record the delicate reds and browns of the autumn leaves. The sketchbook, along with the *Durham N. Shore* sketchbook (TB CLVII), was also used for sketching subjects for the *History of Durham* (see cat.no.26).

Rhine sketchbook 1817

53 **St. Goar, with Rheinfels and Thurnberg.**
The Katz
Pencil
265×404 $(10\frac{7}{16} \times 15\frac{15}{16})$
Turner Bequest; CLXI 27 verso, 28
D12932, D12933

This sketchbook was used on Turner's 1817 tour of the Rhine. It contains numerous pencil sketches on the river from Bingen down to Cologne, many of which were used as the basis for the series of Rhine drawings which were acquired by Fawkes (see cat.nos.29 and 30).

It was the largest sketchbook used on the tour and Turner has made full use of the size to record the expansive views in the Rhineland. He was particularly attracted to the dramatic scenery of St Goar and Rheinfels and the Katz and St Goarhausen on the opposite bank, and had made notes about these places before his journey commenced in the *Itinerary Rhine* sketchbook (TB CLIX) which he used as a guide-book for the tour; 'St. Goar. A small distance below Vessel [Oberwesel] a dangerous Whirlpool a mile below where the bank are very close. Castle of Rhenfels. good Inn. the Bois Verd. Schwalbach water or sour water sold here which corrects the sour wine. The castle of the Cat seen from the Inn ...'. There are numerous other sketches of these places in this book, subjects which formed the basis of several of the Rhine watercolours.

In these drawings, Turner has been careful to note details of local customs such as the costumes of two female figures; he has recorded the mooring of the boats, inscribing the sketch, 'two boats lashed together making one'.

Scotch Antiquities sketchbook 1818

54 **Edinburgh from Calton Hill**
Pencil
112×372 $(4\frac{7}{16} \times 14\frac{5}{8})$
Turner Bequest; CLXVII 39 verso, 40
D13651, D13652

In 1818, Turner was commissioned to make a series of views to illustrate the *Provincial Antiquities of Scotland*, to be published in engraved form with an accompanying text by Sir Walter Scott. At the end of October that year Turner toured Scotland, collecting material for the project. This sketchbook, used on the visit, includes several studies of Edinburgh including this detailed panoramic view of the city which was closely followed in a finished watercolour for the series engraved by George Cooke in 1820 (R.193).

Yorkshire I. sketchbook 1815

55 **Study for the Decline of Carthage**
Pencil
154 × 97 ($6\frac{1}{16} × 3\frac{13}{16}$)
Turner Bequest; CXLIV 101 verso
D11032

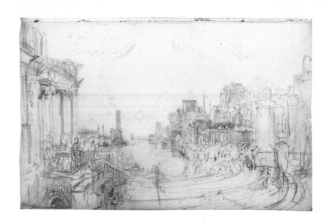

It was the subject-matter of classical mythology and history which inspired Turner to produce some of the most innovative and important paintings of the decade. These include 'Mercury and Herse' (B&J 114), 'Snow Storm: Hannibal and his Army crossing the Alps (B&J 126; Tate Gallery), 'Dido building Carthage' (B&J 131) and the 'Decline of the Carthaginian Empire' (B&J 135; Tate Gallery).

This sketchbook contains several studies for classical or historical pictures including this rough pencil sketch on which the *Decline of the Carthaginian Empire*, of 1817, was clearly based.

Small Roman C. Studies sketchbook 1819

56 **The Colosseum**
Pencil and watercolour on white paper prepared with a grey wash
133 × 255 ($5\frac{3}{16} × 10$)
Turner Bequest; CXC 4
D16398

The majority of the sketchbooks used by Turner in Italy consist entirely of detailed pencil drawings recording every aspect of the country's landscape, architecture and works of art. Only four sketchbooks, of which this is one, contain colour studies and this is the only one of them to have remained intact as a bound sketchbook (see cat.no.32). Like many of the other colour sketches made in Rome, those in this sketchbook are on white paper which has been prepared with an even tonal ground of grey wash. All the drawings in this book are of Rome and the Campagna. Even on so small a scale, Turner has managed to capture the grandeur of the architecture and imbued it with sensitive atmospheric effects.

Skies sketchbook *c.*1818

57 **Study of Sky**
Watercolour
125 × 247 $(4\frac{15}{16} \times 9\frac{11}{16})$
Turner Bequest; CLVIII 41
D12489

This sketchbook contains a series of watercolour studies of cloud effects, sunsets and storms, many of which are extremely beautiful. They are similar in their translucent washes of striking colour combinations to some of the colour studies Turner made of Yorkshire scenery during this decade (see cat. nos. 22 and 24). They may, however, have been made in Italy in 1819 since the sketchbook is the same size and design as the *Small Roman C. Studies* sketchbook (cat.no.56) which contains a few similar studies of cloud effects; Turner's delight in the effects of the Italian light would understandably have inclined him to make careful observation of the sky (see cat.no.33).

Bibliography

All books published in London unless otherwise stated.

Butlin, M. & E. Joll, *The Paintings of J.M.W. Turner*, 2 vols., 1984 (revised edition)

British Museum, *Turner in the British Museum, drawings and watercolours*, exhibition catalogue, 1975

Finberg, A.J., *A Complete Inventory of the Drawings of the Turner Bequest . . .*, 2 vols., 1909

Finberg, A.J., *The History of Turner's 'Liber Studiorum'*, 1924

Finberg, A.J., *The Life of J.M.W. Turner*, 1961 (2nd edition)

Gage, J., *Colour in Turner: Poetry and Truth*, 1969

Hill, D., *In Turner's Footsteps*, 1984

Powell, C., *Turner in the South*, 1987

Rawlinson, W.G., *The Engraved Work of J.M.W. Turner*, 2 vols., 1908–13

Redding, Cyrus, 'The late J.M.W. Turner', *Fraser's Magazine*, XLV, 1852, pp.150–156

Royal Academy of Arts, *Turner 1775–1851*, exhibition catalogue, London, 1974–5

Ruskin, J., *Works* (Library Edition), eds. E.T. Cook and A. Wedderburn, 39 vols., 1903–12

Shanes, E., *Turner's Rivers, Harbours and Coasts*, 1981

Smiles, S., 'Turner in Devon', *Turner Studies*, vol. 7, no. 1, pp.11–13, 1987

Smiles, S., 'The Devonshire Oil Sketches of 1813', *Turner Studies*, vol. 9, no. 1, pp.10–26, 1989

Stainton, L., *Turner's Venice*, 1985

Thornbury, W., *The Life of J.M.W. Turner R.A.*, 2 vols., 1862 (1st edition)

Whitley, W.T. 'Turner as a Lecturer', *Burlington Magazine*, XXII, 1913, pp.202–8

Wilkinson, G., *The Sketches of Turner, R.A.: 1802–1820*, 1974

Wilton, A., *The Life and Work of J.M.W. Turner*, 1979

Wilton, A., *Turner Abroad*, 1982

Wilton, A., *Turner in his Time*, 1987

Wilton, A., *Turner Watercolours in the Clore Gallery*, 1987

York City Art Gallery, *Turner in Yorkshire*, exhibition catalogue, 1980